If God is Good

Why Do We Suffer?

Karyn Henley

Karyn Henley Resources

If God Is Good, Why Do We Suffer?
by Karyn Henley

Copyright © 2007 Karyn Henley. All rights reserved. Exclusively administered by Child Sensitive Communication, LLC.

Cover Photo: © 2007 Jupiterimages Corporation. All rights reserved. Used by permission.

Cover Layout: Ralph Henley

The dandelion logo is a trademark of Karyn Henley.

For permission to copy excerpts from this book, contact office@karynhenley.com.

Unless otherwise indicated all Scripture quotations are taken from the Holy Bible, New International Version®. NIV®. Copyright © 1973, 1978, 1984 by International Bible Society. Used by permission of Zondervan Publishing House. All rights reserved.

No part of this publication may be reproduced, stored in a retrieval syustem, or transmitted in any form or by any means (electronic, mechanical, photocopying, recording, or otherwise) without prior written permission.

ISBN 1-9338030-18-5

Table of Contents

1.

Just Wondering . . .

"The statistics on death are quite impressive. One out of one people die."

- George Bernard Shaw [1]

Just Wondering . . .

In 2001, there was a total eclipse of my birthday. A very modest and ordinary date, September 11, used to come before my birthday. Now I know of my birthday as the day after 9/11.

Maybe each generation can point to a defining day, a day that brought them face to face with evil, a day that's seared in the collective memory. For my parents, it was no doubt the day Pearl Harbor was attacked, the day that will forever "live in infamy," the day the world took a detour and never came back.

Then there was the assasination of President Kennedy which, because of the tv cameras, happened before our very eyes. The fallout of that event was not as globally tragic as Pearl Harbor, but for our nation, it was a major speed bump. None of my generation will ever forget exactly where we were when we were stunned with the news.

Nor will we ever forget the shock of 9/11, when the whole world witnessed a hemispheric head-on collision.

Of course, all along, each of us has taken hits that left us reeling while our neighbors went merrily on their way. My beloved grandmother died of cancer when I was 12, and my personal world was never the same. When I was in junior high, a classmate was killed in a car crash. She was only an acquaintance, but I still remember the shock. Then the year after my younger son was born, my one-year-old nephew died during a surgery meant to correct a heart problem. At the funeral, I held my own healthy baby in my arms, grieving that my sister's arms were empty. Last year, a dear friend was killed in a freak freeway accident. He left a pregnant wife and four children. You, too, carry your own pain and griefs, different from mine, but just as deep.

Then there's media-induced pain. News clips and magazine articles show us the plights of people we don't even know. At the least, we cringe. Or we're appalled. Occasionally we're outraged enough to do something to right the wrong, to try to alleviate the suffering. Of course, I guess some of us are so accustomed to hearing bad news, we don't even feel the shock of it anymore. The media shows us disaster after disaster, most of which we might never have known about if we had lived before the information-saturated, global age.

I guess we can't totally blame the media, though. Suffering and disaster draw viewers. Something in us wants to hear about other people's pain. Novelists know they have to write about characters working their way through situations that go from bad to worse to how-will-they-ever-get-out-of-this. Otherwise, no one will want to read their books. It's the same with non-fiction. We're interested in people's dilemmas, their problems, their tragedies. We want to know how they handled the hard stuff. Or maybe we feel better knowing someone else is worse off than we are. Maybe we find comfort in the fact that we're not alone in suffering, that if someone else slogged through the Swamp of Despair, we can too.

But sometimes I find that I've collected other people's fear and grief and pain, and I've carried it around as part of my own baggage. That's part of the insidiousness of evil. It can terrify us, stop us in our tracks, torment us, even if it's not touching us directly. Either way – whether it's an evil that has rocked the planet or simply the pain of my small individual world – it haunts my mind with one question:

Why, God, why?

N.T. Wright says we ignore evil "when it doesn't hit us in the face, and so we are shocked and puzzled when it does." [2] If you're like me, you'd like to ignore evil. Maybe we think if we ignore it, it will go away. Maybe we feel totally helpless to do anything about it. Maybe one reason we don't often ask the Why is because if we ask such a question, people might think we're doubting God. Well, count me in as one of the shocked and puzzled. I can't ignore the question anymore. It roars in my brain. Deafens my thoughts. Shakes its fist in the face of my old pat answers.

So you could say this book is for the shocked and puzzled, for people like me asking the Why question. School shootings, child molesting, suicide bombings – why, God, why? Devastating tornadoes, tsunamis, hurricanes – why, God, why? Inoperable cancer, Alzheimer's, a child's terminal illness – why, God, why? Didn't you know this was coming, God? If you did, couldn't you have stopped it? If you could have stopped it, why didn't you?

Why pain? Why suffering? Why evil? People who don't believe in God don't ask this question, of course. What's more, if you don't believe in one loving, caring God, the question doesn't bother you, because you see evil as simply our human condition. We're born, grow up, grow old, get sick, and die. That's how we escape. We die.

But for people who believe in a personal, loving, caring God, the Why question is very real. And it has niggled at the hearts of believers for centuries. No – make that millenia. The Why question has been around since before the time of Job. Scholars have chewed it up and spit it out over and over again to the point of turning the Why into a branch of study called, in scholarly verbiage, "theodicy." In Greek, "theos" means God, and "dike" means judgment or justice. So theodicy means "justice of God." Theodicy deals with reconciling two seemingly disparate concepts: a good, loving, powerful God and a world of suffering and evil.

Now if the Why question has been around for millenia, it doesn't take much of a brain to see that no one's discovered the big BECAUSE to answer the big WHY. We're no closer now to pinpointing a definite answer than we were when we carried clubs and wore lionskin. So you might ask another Why: Why muck through this swamp again? Why ponder the undefinable? Why ask the unanswerable?

Here's my Because: It seems to me that if you believe in a good, loving God, you owe yourself an honest quest for some explanation of the presence of suffering and evil. But maybe you're satisfied with where you are spiritually, and you don't want to rock your boat. Then I say you owe an explanation to the people in your life who need and crave a loving God. Presumably you are going to assure them that God is good. God is love. God is all-powerful. But evil, suffering, and pain seem to stand as undeniable evidence against the existence of a good, loving, all-powerful God.

So how do you explain it to yourself? What's more, how do you explain it to your children, your friend, your co-worker? What do you say to a believer teetering on the edge of disbelief? That may in fact describe you. Many people have reported going through a "dark night of the soul," in which they asked themselves the Why, or at least the Why-Me.

Classic faith-growth studies show that people who have been raised to believe in a loving God take their belief for granted for awhile. Maybe for a long while. We start out imitating the signs of faith of the significant people in our lives. As we grow, we begin to identify with a faith community and its beliefs. Our community's stories of faith become a part of our own faith.[3] Here's where some people stop. They live their whole lives at this stage. They don't question what they've been taught, so they continue to take their beliefs for granted for the rest of their lives.

But it's natural, even healthy, to question what we believe. This stage of questioning, when it occurs naturally, usually appears in early adolescence and lasts into young adulthood. But some young adults hang onto the taken-for-grantedness of their faith. They don't question until their beliefs are challenged – maybe by the Why when it slaps them in the face.

Whether we question our faith naturally or because of a challenge, the very act of questioning indicates that we've dropped the taken-for-grantedness and we're trying to personalize our faith. In essence, we're asking, "Is this truly my personal faith, or is it my friend's? Is this what I really believe, or just what I was taught to believe?"

A healthy faith continues to exercise its muscles. Some people are afraid that what they believe will melt under the heat of scrutiny, so they pack it in ice and stash it away and post a "Do Not Enter" sign. They're right. That kind of faith will die if it's even peeked at. Because it's not really their faith. They've just co-opted it. That kind of faith is not healthy.

In order to personalize faith and maintain a healthy faith, we have to be able to ask questions and arrive at answers that make sense to us, even if the answers include, "I don't think I'll ever be certain about that issue." It is, of course, possible to move forward toward maturity while living in uncertainty. People do it all the time. In fact, that's part of what maturity is: being able to live with uncertainty. But there's a difference between being uncertain with your eyes closed and being uncertain with your eyes wide open. At least with your eyes wide open, you can see a lot farther.

Faith-growth experts say we mature in faith by a process: We question what we believe, we wrestle with it, we come to a more confident stance in our beliefs, and we move ahead with that stance. Then we hit another question, and the process starts over again. To me, this process is like climbing up and around a mountain. Questions lead us along our path. We circle around the mountain again and again, and our faith matures. Every time we go around the mountain, we reach a higher elevation. Our horizons expand. Our view broadens.

Of course, at times the path leads into cloud cover, and we can't see anything at all. Or we find ourselves in a sudden storm that threatens to pour us over the cliff in a ton of mud. Or we have to pick our way through a rockslide that has obliterated the way. Or we just grow weary and wonder why we ever started this climb in the first place. We may camp out for awhile. At any rate, questions continue to pop up. A healthy faith is honest enough to see the questions and ponder them and come up with an answer or two or ten.

I think the Why question is inevitable. It's at the core of one of the most powerful arguments for atheists: If God were all-powerful, He could stop all this suffering. If He were good, loving, and caring, He would stop it. That means either He's not all-powerful, or He's not good, loving, and caring. Therefore, atheists reason, what you call "God" does not exist.

Good point. Very good point. But I question the validity of that verdict. Consider for a moment: In a court of law, the accused is innocent unless his guilt is proved beyond a reasonable doubt. So if God is the accused – if God is the one on trial here – maybe the question to ask is whether there's a plausible explanation for why a good, loving, all-powerful God would allow so much suffering in this world.

I mentioned earlier that the Why is a problem only for people who believe in a loving, all-powerful God. Buddhists don't have to worry about theodicy. Classic Buddhism is basically atheistic already. Besides, the Buddhists' whole foundational premise is that the world is suffering. They point to the suffering of the world to explain why they strive to be released from it.

Hindus don't have to worry about theodicy, because they have thousands of gods and goddesses, which they believe to be incarnations of their one highest reality. The point is, some of these gods are good and some are evil. It's a given that evil gods and goddesses can wreak all kinds of havoc among humans.

It's the same with Shintoism. Some of their myriads of gods (kami) are good, some are evil, and some are both – good at times and evil at times.

Taoists (Daoists) don't have to worry about theodicy, because they view all opposites as interrelated and necessary: light and dark, up and down, good and evil. The solution to suffering is to live in harmony with this natural balance of the world.

Deists don't have to worry about theodicy, because they don't believe God is near or personally involved. He made the world, then left it to run on its own devices.

Muslims don't worry about theodicy, because although God is powerful, He is not love. He is authoritarian, demanding, and vengeful.

But Christians believe and proclaim, "God is love" (1 John 4:8). "For God so loved the world, He gave His only Son" (John 3:16). "A new commandment I give you: Love one another. As I have loved you, so you must love one another" (John 13:34). So can we explain, first of all to ourselves, this good-God/suffering-world dilemma? Is there a plausible explanation?

As it turns out, there are several plausible explanations. Any one of them – or some combination of them – may be right. At the least, plausible explanations give us a reason to suspect that God is not non-existent, nor is He impotent, nor is He unloving and uncaring. The following chapters lay out the options, at least the ones I've discovered in my trek around the mountain. From the outset, let me say that I'm not going to give you all these options and then proclaim which one is the answer. Some of the explanations make more sense to me than others. But I don't know the exact answer. And I certainly wouldn't presume to tell you what to believe. I'll simply try to lead us to some place of hope as we explore. So . . . care to join me for a turn or two around the mountain?

2.

Mystery

"The God of Genesis, a God I recognize, is inexplicable. . . . . I try to be glad for . . . the times we don't get what we deserve, but better. I never ask, for instance, why Mother Teresa is dead and I'm alive, why my friend Paul was killed by brain cancer, and although I am much less good and useful, I was not."

- A. L. Kennedy [1]

"Reverend Marshall . . . said we could never truly understand God's will. We have to trust God, have faith in Him, and follow the rules He gave us without ever understanding Him. . . . Maybe when we're in Heaven we'll understand, but until then all we can do is pray for His forgiveness and obey His will."

- Megan,
character in <u>Life As We Knew It</u> [2]

Option 1: Evil is a Mystery

I recently visited Egypt with a Jewish friend who was researching a book on Jews in Egypt during World War II. She tried to get interviews with the few Jews who still live there and were alive during the 1930's and 1940's, but they were all reluctant to talk. Our experience confirmed what Professor Luke Timothy Johnson reports: After the Holocaust, Jewish people went into "a post-traumatic silence." Dr. Johnson says a common belief among Holocaust survivors was: "It is impertinent to talk about God; it is blasphemous to talk about theology in light of the Holocaust." [3]

So many people are silent on the subject of theodicy that I suspect many of them fall back on the position that it's impertinent to ask. It's just not up to us to say. It's a mystery, a paradox. If this is your belief, you are in scholarly company. Saint Bernard of Clairvaux called Why questions about God "scandalous curiosity." [4] Soren Kierkegaard, a devout Christian and dedicated philosopher, believed that a great many tenets of Christianity had to be accepted by what he called "a leap of faith."

That's definitely one way to look at it. Many people are fine, thank you very much, living with that non-explanatory explanation. That reminds me of a poem written by Mary Oliver, a Pulitzer-prize winning poet. In one poem, she muses about a mockingbird and says that perhaps it already has enough knowledge "to be perfectly content not knowing." [5]   In the end, after turning the good-God/suffering-world conundrum inside out and upside down, that might be exactly where you end up. In fact, it might be where I end up.

Maybe the important issue is why we choose this option.   As I pointed out before, some people are afraid their faith will melt under hot questions. Or they think asking questions would offend God. Or they think questions might portray them as doubters or two-faced. Maybe they feel asking "why" would be a betrayal of the original commitment from which they promised never to turn back.

I respect that. But as you know, for me, questioning is just another circle around the mountain to a higher level. If God is the Creator, and if God was pleased with the humans He made (He said "It is very good"), then it seems to me He was pleased with the way humans think and wonder and question.   Randall Niles, in What Happened to Me?, says, "Faith is not about turning off the brain and merely relying on the heart, or squashing reason in favor of emotion." [6]   One postmodern points out that when her generation hears people advise them to "just believe," they hear it as, "don't think." [7]

Not daring to question God is a prominent feature of Islam. To Muslims, God's sovereignty is unchallengeable. As Daniel Boorstin explains the Muslim view: "Who was man to make suffering a 'problem' when it was simply a fact of Allah's creation?" [8]   So Muslims don't question Allah or the Qur'an, "the book in which there is no doubt." The major doubt that hangs over all Muslims is the question of eternity. Will this sovereign, unchallengeable God, in the end, allow me to enter heaven or consign me to a cruel hell? Obviously, this picture of God does not include gracious, self-giving love.

As I pointed out before, Buddhists don't question suffering either. Buddha's "Fire Sermon" says: "Bhikkus, all is burning.. . . . Burning with what? Burning with the fire of lust, with the fire of hate, with the fire of delusion." And according to the Buddhist principle of "skillful means," any means used to get people to escape suffering, including lies and deceit, is justifiable. [9]

Christians don't believe in using lies and deceit, but we sometimes have a similar view of life: Everything is bad and full of suffering, and we have to help people come to Jesus so they can escape to heaven someday. Unlike Buddhists, of course, we claim an all-powerful, loving God. That brings us back to the Why.

It also brings us to another important question. What are we talking about: pain? suffering? death? evil? So far I've pretty much tumbled them all together. And it's true that evil involves pain, suffering, and death. But do pain, suffering, and death always involve evil? Perhaps a test might be to ask whether the situation leads to life and love or whether it leads to destruction and ruin. Of course, if you push this test too far, you end up siding with the utilitarian philosophers, who suggested judging what was right by asking what would bring the greatest good for the greatest number of people. Which reminds me of what Caiaphas, the high priest, said: "It is better for you that one man die for the people than that the whole nation perish." Of course, that one man was innocent. [10]

Maybe one of my experiences with pain will help illuminate the pain/evil question. I held my infant grandson while a nurse drew blood from his heel to give him a blood test he needed. I knew the procedure would cause him pain. I aided and abetted in the perpetration of that pain. But nothing about the situation was evil. The purpose was for good. It was a reasonable act.

In contrast, there's something unreasonable about evil. It seems to have no purpose except destruction and hurt. Evil has no remorse. At least that's the way it seems. And that brings us back full circle to the Why. If evil is totally destructive, remorseless, and unreasonable, then why does God allow it?

Could evil be just a shadow, a phantom that disturbs me only because I don't understand it from God's point of view? If evil is nothing (which, by the way, may be what Tolkein believed [11]), then it truly is a horror. It's a macabre absurdity, a hideous distortion of life, a fun-house mirror that's no fun.

Of course, God the Creator is, by definition, far greater than creation. And I am definitely part of creation. Which makes my attempts to figure God out look like an exercise in futility. The depths of God's understanding are unfathomable. The heights of God's wisdom are unscalable. If I trust God, I must say that He reveals to me not all I want to know, but all I need to know. So if God has not revealed the answer to the Why, maybe I'm not supposed to know. God certainly doesn't owe me an explanation of everything that piques my curiosity.

On the other hand, God encourages us to seek, so I can only assume that there's some benefit in the seeking, some curve in the mountain path that will open a new vista that verifies again His reality and goodness and power.

So why evil, suffering, and pain? Option #1: "It's an unsolvable mystery, a paradox we can't understand.

Only God knows." Can we live with that answer? Does it stand up to the questioning world? Can we be satisfied with a shrug of the shoulders?

Mystery and paradox may be our answer in the end. But since we're just on square one, it doesn't seem right that we should simply leave our token here. Shouldn't we go around the board before we end up back at square one – if indeed that's where we end up? So roll the die, flip the coin, draw the card. Where do we go next?

3.

Wrath

"But it's impossible for me – impossible – to believe that there is anything that could be described as a loving God who could allow what happens in our world daily."

- Chuck Templeton [1]

Option 2: We Suffer Because of God's Wrath

As I mentioned earlier, Hindus believe in a whole pantheon of gods and goddesses, all emanations of their one reality, Brahman. These gods and goddesses are filled with human-like passions. So, while some of these deities are good, some are evil. Mark W. Muesse, professor of comparative religions at Rhodes College, points out, ". . . epidemics, such as smallpox . . . are viewed as the result of the goddess's anger at being neglected by her village or patrons. . . . sufferings one endures in this life are regarded as the chastisements of an ultimately loving mother, to whom one clings in all circumstances." [2] Suffering is the result of a deity's wrath.

Muslims often attribute disasters to God's wrath. A recent magazine article told how a professor in Islamabad, after the terrible 2005 earthquake in Kashmir, explained to his students the geological process of the earthquake. He told them the earthquake was caused by the movement of tectonic plates. Around the room, students held up their hands and corrected him. They insisted that the earthquake was the result of God's wrath. [3]

This story reminded me of comments I've heard from some Christians. After a tornado ripped through downtown Nashville, Tennessee (where I live), several prophetic voices explained that this disaster was a sign of

God's judgment on us. A similar explanation came out after 9/11. Pat Robertson and Jerry Falwell pointed at the sins of the U.S. culture and said the attacks that day were God's punishment; the U.S. was getting what it deserved. [4] And when a top official in the Middle-East became critically ill, a high-profile Christian in the West proclaimed that the official's illness was God's judgment.

Of course, this is a valid explanation for the why-evil question. On the other hand, does it explain the good-God side of the dilemma? It might instead make us question God's goodness.

The God's wrath option is made plausible, I suppose, by the way God is portrayed in the Old Testament. He's the eye-for-an-eye, tooth-for-a-tooth God. (Although maybe we need to realize that the mandated eye-for-an-eye was actually a merciful rule, because at that time in history, if you poked out somebody's eye, their tribe would swoop down on yours and kill the whole lot of you. Anyone who escaped would likely carry a vendetta until he could get revenge. Unfortunately, we don't have to look into history to know how this works.)

A Chinese proverb says, "If you seek revenge, dig two graves." [5] Maybe that's what God was trying to get us to avoid when He said, "Vengeance is mine, I will repay." [6] How does God get revenge anyway? God's revenge is inhuman: He takes the hit. Look at the cross.

When the apostle Paul quoted this God's-vengeance passage in his letter to the Romans, he followed it by saying, "If your enemies are hungry, feed them; if they are thirsty, give them something to drink . . ." [7] He went on to say, "Do not be overcome by evil, but overcome evil with good." In essence, he was saying, "Leave retribution to God. Otherwise, you'll be overcome by evil, perpetrating it in yourself as you try to get revenge."

Deep in the human psyche is the sense of payback. Hindus and Buddhists call this concept karma. It's the cause and effect of human action: We reap what we sow. What goes around comes around. You get what's coming to you. It's a natural principle that seems to be built into us. When we work overtime, we know we deserve overtime pay. When we overeat, we know we deserve the stomach ache.

But Hindu and Buddhist karma goes further. The good you do (good karma) earns good merits. The bad you do (bad karma) garners demerits. Then after death, you reincarnate in a body and situation that's determined by the karma of your previous life. So if you're Hindu or Buddhist, you blame your suffering on the bad karma of your past life. Your present suffering is believed to be a form of punishment that must be experienced to the full.

A recent mission report from Central Asia shows the effects of this view of karma. It told about mothers of disabled children who wept as they recounted the times relatives and neighbors had blamed the children's disabilities on the mothers, accusing them of harboring a hidden sin or spiritual deficiency or an evil nature. Another recent example comes from southern Korea. A ferris wheel car turned over, dumping five members of one family to their deaths. "Too bad," a man commented. "They probably deserved it." That's the concept of karma at work.

Of course, Christians don't believe in reincarnation. But we do have a sense of justice. We know we should get what we deserve. Even Christians ask things like, "What sin in our midst caused God to send this drought?" There's a common belief that when we suffer in this life, we're being punished or disciplined by God. We can reconcile this with the good-God/suffering-world dilemma if we think of God as a loving Father who disciplines us. The writer of the Hebrew letter says, "Endure hardship as discipline; God is treating you as sons. For what son is not disciplined by his father?" [8]

But does God cause, or allow, my innocent baby to suffer in order to discipline me? If I get cancer, should I look around and ask what I did wrong – why is God punishing me? Is all suffering the result of punishment or discipline? It seems that if we answer yes, we'll need to be ready to defend the goodness and love of God.

Let's think about discipline for a minute. Studies in the field of behavior management tell us that the most effective discipline is appropriate to the misbehavior. For one thing, the best discipline relates to what was done. Then, too, the degree of the discipline fits the offense. In other words, if a child carelessly spills her milk, the discipline may be for her to clean up her own spill. But if Dad tells her to set the glass of milk by the sink and she deliberately throws it across the room instead, the consequence is understandably more serious.

Effective discipline is also meted out close to the time of the misbehavior. And a good, loving parent will be consistent in discipline. He won't be erratic, sometimes punishing a certain misbehavior but ignoring it at other times. What's more, as parents, we are counseled to let ourselves cool down if we're angry, so we won't overreact and discipline too heavily. It seems to me that God's discipline will be at least as good as that of a loving earthly parent. Which means His discipline will be consistent, timely, no harsher than necessary, and appropriate to the situation.

There's a variation to our question then: Does God instigate the suffering in order to discipline us, or does God use the painful circumstances of our lives as natural teachers and correctors? Natural consequences usually pay us back quite well, and they're already built into the way the world operates. So maybe God rarely has to intervene. Maybe that's why suffering is built into the world in the first place.

Still, if someone says the fender-bender they had this afternoon was God's way of punishing them for the lie they told last week, I have a hard time believing them. I've heard strong Christians talk this way. It doesn't make much sense to me, though, to say all the innocent suffering in the world is due to God punishing us. Besides, as I understand it, Jesus took our punishment.

Let's explore this discipline-punishment concept a little further. We humans do believe that bad people should suffer or at least get their due. Anyone with a sense of justice believes that people acting unjustly must be stopped. So if God is just, He will have to deal with those who perpetuate evil. He can't let them off the hook as if their actions didn't matter.

As I write this, I'm sitting in a hotel room in Austin, Texas. My husband and I walked to a nearby restaurant for dinner this evening. When we left the hotel, a young man dashed out past us, and a girl screamed, "He stole my purse!" A couple of her friends, athletic-type guys, sprinted after the thief. They tackled him about a block away. You can bet that young man is in big trouble. And he should be. We all know that bad people should suffer. C.S. Lewis wrote, "Until the evil man finds evil unmistakably present in his existence in the form of pain, he is enclosed in illusion. Once pain has roused him, he knows that he is in some way or other 'up against' the real universe." [9]

But the truth is, evil people are not always punished. They don't always suffer. It's often innocent people who suffer. That's the subject of the Bible's book of Job. It's the original book on theodicy. It's a long book, but basically it goes like this:

God gives Satan permission to destroy everything in Job's life. (Hmmm. A sinister twist on suffering. We'll come back to this in the next chapter.) Raiders attack, steal all Job's livestock, and kill his servants. Then a whirlwind hits the house where Job's children are gathered, killing them all. If that's not bad enough, Job himself is struck with a devastating skin disease.

In the wake of all this disaster, four of Job's friends come to visit him. What do they think of all this suffering? What does Job think? Here's a mini-version:

Eliphaz: Do not despise the chastising of the Almighty when you sin. (4:17, 18)
Job: Stop assuming my guilt, for I am righteous. . . . Don't I know the difference between right and wrong?" (6:29, 30)

Bildad: Your children obviously sinned against God, so their punishment was well-deserved. (8:4)
Job: Who am I that I should try to answer God or even reason with him? (9:14)

Zophar: God is doubtless punishing you far less than you deserve. (11:16)
Job: You are smearing me with lies. (13:4)

Elihu: It was to prevent you from getting into a life of evil that God sent this suffering.
(36:21)

God: Who is this that questions my wisdom with such ignorant words?" (38:2) Do you still want to argue with the Almighty? You are God's critic, but do you have the answers? (40:1)

God to Eliphaz: I am angry with you and your two friends, for you have not been right in what you said about me. . . . I will not treat you as you deserve, for you have not been right in what you said about me." (42:7, 8)

Basically, Job's friends claimed he was suffering because did something wrong. "Come on and admit it," they said. But Job said, "I'm innocent." And God agreed. In fact, God didn't even give Eliphaz what he deserved for accusing Job falsely. Why? To prove His point: He doesn't make us suffer in order to punish us. At least not in Job's case.

So option #2: We suffer because of God's wrath. Do we?

But, speaking of Job's case, let's go back to one of the strands we touched a while ago, one of the strange and disturbing aspects of Job's story. The Accuser. Satan.

4.

Satan

"The LORD said to Satan, 'Where have you come from?' Satan answered the LORD, 'From roaming through the earth and going back and forth in it.'"

- Job 1:7

Option 3: We Suffer Because of Satan

Many religions attribute evil to demonic forces or evil spirits. Among the Hindu pantheon of gods and goddesses, some are attributed with the powers and wisdom to defend and protect the world from demons. Others are blamed for creating disasters in their anger.

Animists, too, believe evil spirits cause suffering.. Ken Rideout, longtime missionary to Thailand, gives an example:

A field worker comes home sick one day. So he goes to the shaman of the village. The shaman asks which tree the worker urinated on that day. When the worker tells him, the head man prescribes the remedy for his illness: Present a bowl of glutinous rice, some fruit, maybe some whiskey to the demon of the tree, because the demon was offended when he urinated on the tree. Then the demon won't make the man sick anymore, says the shaman. [1]

Good and evil are central to the teaching of Zoroastrianism. In this religion, there are two supreme beings, one good and the other evil. These two powers are equal and independent of each other, and they fight over the world. The job of humans is to join the side of good so that good will eventually overpower evil and win the war over the earth.

Some Christians come very close to this same type of dualism. Just a few days ago, I heard an evangelist say that the battle is over our souls. God versus Satan. In many churches, sermons are specifically designed to strengthen the congregants to battle on the side of God, to "storm the gates of hell," to fight the unseen powers and principalities of evil. But unlike Zoroastrianism, Christianity teaches that Jesus has struck the fatal blow, and the end of the story is assured: God wins and Satan is defeated, with or without our help. Still, it seems that Satan often gets the upper hand in our world.

So one explanation for evil is that before humans were created, a being – possibly an angel, maybe a quasi-being [2] – rebelled against God and wormed himself into the position of ruler of the demons who joined his revolt. Maybe. That theory is pieced together from several strange Bible verses that are never explained completely. In addition, <u>The Book of Enoch</u>, widely read by the Jews before and during the time of Christ, details the fall of Satan and even names over twenty fallen angels.[3] The fourteenth century poet Dante imagined an entire hellish "Inferno" in his <u>Divine Comedy</u> from the idea that Lucifer (another name for Satan) and other angels revolted and were thrown down into the center of the earth. Or maybe this anti-good being was originally created to be in charge of a hell-like realm never meant for humans, but he/it overstepped his/its bounds. Only God knows.

New Testament writers talk about Satan too, often referring to him/it as "the devil." He/it is blamed for disease not only in Job, but also by Luke the physician [4] and Jesus:

"Then should not this (deformed) woman, . . . whom Satan has kept bound for eighteen long years, be set free on the Sabbath day from what bound her?" Jesus asked. [5]

The New Testament shows Satan to be a tempter who targets even Jesus. He/it does not "have in mind the things of God, but the things of men." From some people, he/it "takes away the word that was sown in them." Satan entered some people, as did evil or "unclean" spirits, also known as "demons," who are commonly thought to be his/its "angels." Satan wants to "sift" people "like wheat" – note that the "you" in the passage is plural. The devil is called an enemy.

Jesus said He "saw Satan fall like lightning from heaven" and said he/it "was a murderer from the beginning, not holding to the truth, for there is no truth in him. When he lies, he speaks his native language, for he is a liar and the father of lies." The apostle Paul characterized the devil as being "full of all kinds of deceit and trickery" and "perverting the right ways of the Lord." [6]

In short, all sorts of disasters are blamed on Satan and demons, and this seems to be a plausible reason for evil. The good news is that before Jesus was crucified, He said, "Now is the time for judgment on this world; now the prince of this world will be driven out." The apostle John, who reported this, also wrote, "The reason the Son of God appeared was to destroy the devil's work." [7]

But the reality is that while we do experience some healings and other miracles even today, we also experience plenty of suffering. Which leaves us with the Why plus an add-on: If Jesus came to destroy the work of the devil and drive out the prince of the world, why is evil still around? Why does it seem just as potent as ever? If God is more powerful than the devil and his/its hordes, then obviously God has given them the freedom to cause their evil. So it looks as though we're living between the declaration of the devil's demise and its completion. In which case, I echo Habakkuk: "How long, O Lord?" [8]

Now, just to throw a kink into this line of thought: The word translated "Satan" is really "the satan," which means "the accuser." So we could reason that Jesus came to destroy the work of the accuser, who is prince of the world. (We earth-bound beings do like to point the finger and lay blame.) It makes total sense that Jesus came to free us from accusation, because it's accusation that condemns us, and in Jesus there is no condemnation. There's no amassing of good deeds or karma by which we earn God's love, no tallying of bad deeds or karma by which we incur God's wrath. John wrote that Jesus didn't come into the world to condemn the world.[9] So it makes sense that some people take "Satan" symbolically.

"Satan" is possibly both a being (or quasi-being) and a symbol for the destructive effect of accusation. But I personally can't relegate "the evil one" totally to symbol-ism, because when I was in college I saw something too real to explain away. I was worshiping in a small group in an acquaintance's living room, when a classmate began to scream out in a deep, male voice. This classmate was female. Believe me, she could not have manufactured this voice. It freaked us all out. You might say it literally scared the hell out of the rest of us. By God's grace, some-one at this meeting had dealt with these things before and was able to step in and exert God's authority.

Anyway, whether personal, quasi-personal, or symbolic, Satan is one option to explain evil, and one that lots of people choose. This option, however, almost poses more questions than it answers. In addition to the question of why we still experience evil if Jesus defeated Satan at the cross, other questions pop up. Where did the accuser come from? If God created everything, did He create the accuser, too? And if God is stronger, why didn't he just snuff out the accuser the first time he/it accused or perpetrated evil? If we're trying to answer the good-God/suffering-world dilemma, doesn't this put the responsibility back on God? So the Why question is still open.

5.

God

"I well knew that he (God) who bound me (with sickness) so painfully would unbind me when he wished."
- Julian of Norwich [1]

Option 4: God Produces Both Good and Evil

Related to the thoughts we might have about Satan's role in Job's suffering is the question of why Satan came with the angels when they presented themselves before the Lord. In Hebrew, the word "angels" means "sons of God." So why was Satan allowed into God's courts, into God's presence with the "sons of God"? Was Satan welcome there? Was he/it one of the angels? Had he/it been given responsibility over the more painful aspects of life? Even if the story of Job is a symbolic tale through which the people of Israel grappled with the question of evil, it poses another option: God produces both good and evil at His divine discretion.

Other biblical passages might support this notion: "God sent an evil spirit between Abimelech and the citizens of Shechem, who acted treacherously against Abimelech." (Judges 9:23, 24)

"Now the Spirit of the LORD had departed from Saul, and an evil spirit (or 'injurious spirit') from the LORD tormented him" (1 Samuel 16:14)

"The next day an evil spirit from God came forcefully upon Saul." (1 Samuel 18:10)

The question is, did God actually send the evil spirit from His own entourage of heavenly hosts? Or did He summon an evil spirit from its shadowy abode and make it do His bidding on these occasions? Or did God simply allow the evil spirit to operate freely in these people's lives?

Then there are the lying spirits. The prophet Micaiah reported seeing God on his throne surrounded by a heavenly host. God asked, "Who will entice Ahab into attacking Ramoth Gilead and going to his death there?" Different heavenly beings suggested different ways to entice Ahab. "Finally, a spirit came forward, stood before the LORD and said, 'I will entice him.' 'By what means?' the LORD asked. 'I will go out and be a lying spirit in the mouths of all his prophets,' he said." Micaiah reported, "So now the LORD has put a lying spirit in the mouths of all these prophets of yours. The LORD has decreed disaster for you" (1 Kings 22:19-23).

Are these good spirits that are lying only when God tells them to? Or are they evil spirits who are allowed by God to operate only in certain situations?

When God first tells Moses to approach Pharaoh with the demand that he let the Israelites leave Egypt, Moses protests that he's not an eloquent speaker. God says, "Who gave man his mouth? Who makes him deaf or mute? Who gives him sight or makes him blind? Is it not I, the LORD?" (Exodus 4:10-11). If suffering includes deafness, muteness, and blindness, this statement is thought-provoking.

The question now becomes: Can a loving God send both evil and good, both suffering and comfort? That's a belief called Monism. C.S. Lewis explains that in Monism, "God Himself, being 'above good and evil,' produces impartially the effects to which we give those two names." [2]

As I said earlier, if we don't believe that God is love – or if we don't believe that God is all-powerful – this is no problem. In religions like Hinduism, God is viewed as the source of both good and evil. In that case, Mark Muesse points out, "evil is a practical problem, not a theological one." [3] In other words, the world is the way it is, God includes all of it, and we have to deal with it.

As in Hinduism, secular philosophy sees good and evil as two faces of the same world. But Hinduism has deities and secular philosophy does not. Modern philosophy in the West discounted God, but found it still had to deal with the practical problem of evil. So modernism focused on progress to rid us of suffering and evil. Modernists knew that there would, naturally, be some suffering along this road, but it was all for the betterment of humankind as progress rolled toward its bright destination. [4]

But modernism is being rapidly swallowed by postmodernism, because we saw that modernism's destination doesn't look so bright. We're thinking more now about the mystical and spiritual, and – well – questions like: Could God encompass both good and evil? Could perfect love and suffering both be part of the same divine mind?

Maybe we should examine our definition of love. Maybe I'm wrong if I think that a good, loving God shouldn't allow me to hurt at all, not the teensiest bit. I think back to how immature I was when I graduated from high school. (I would say stupid, but I'm trying to be a bit kind to myself here.) I ask myself: How have I grown more mature since then? (Assuming I've matured.) The answer is that I've had to work through pain and problems. If I look ahead and ask how I'm going to grow to be more mature in the future, the answer would be: pain and problems. Suffering. Hmmm . . .

Maybe, too, the good-God/suffering-world dilemma depends on how we define suffering. If we wanted to rid the world of suffering, how far would we go? To my way of thinking, abuse and sickness would disappear. Would we take away the pain and sweat of exercise? The challenges of everyday life? What would happen to life? I don't ask these questions to bring us to a definite conclusion; I'm just wondering aloud.

Another question: Can you imagine this world without pain? When the dentist numbs your gums, he or she warns you not to chew or eat until the numbness wears off. Why? Because you could bite your tongue or the inside of your cheek and never know it. Pain warns us not to get too close to fire. The memory of a wasp sting warns us to back off when we see wasps swarming. A prick tells us to let go of a piece of broken glass. Or a twinge of pain in a tooth says there's something wrong that needs to be taken care of. A backache, a stomach ache, a headache, can be signs that we need to take better care of our bodies and even our minds.

Then there are times when we endure pain for a greater good. When I was a child, I hated the pain of shots. Fuss and cry as I might, my mother was never moved to back down. I got all my inoculations on schedule. Yet I don't doubt her love for me. Frankly, the greatest pain I've ever experienced was in childbirth. But I endured it for the sake of the new life coming into the world, and I've never regretted it. As a parent, I let my babies fall down plenty of times while they were learning to walk. I only intervened when I saw that the danger was too great for them to handle.

In all these instances, the love and the pain swirl together as unified elements of the same experience. So when we say, "Why would a loving God . . . ," maybe that "loving" does not preclude pain and suffering. When we say, "Why would He allow evil and suffering," maybe that "evil" and "suffering" does not preclude the purposes of love, especially omniscient love.

The philosopher Kierkegaard saw "pain, sickness, frustration, death" as "the experience that alerted and awakened man to his existence." [5] If that's the case, I can see that it's plausible that God might serve up both evil and good.

One of the dreads of the human life is death. The Bible often calls death an enemy, as when the apostle Paul wrote, "The last enemy to be destroyed is death." [6] But we also know that some of us welcome death. The writer Ralph C. Wood reports that Tolkein saw death "as one of our greatest gifts." [7] Wood says, "The fact that life is shadowed by death does not make it (death) evil. On the contrary, the omnipresence of death renders life immensely precious" [8]

A few years ago, I found a recipe for chocolate cake that looked good except for one ingredient: vinegar. I hate the smell of vinegar. So the first time I made the cake, I hesitated before adding it. Could this be an error in the recipe? Did they really mean vinegar? But I added it in spite of my doubts. The result was one of the most delicious chocolate cakes I've ever eaten.

So maybe God has a firm grasp on both good and evil, both love and suffering. Maybe good and evil are thoroughly mixed, at least in the framework of a time-bound world. In the next chapter, we'll begin exploring why that might be. For now, let's sum up where we are at this point. If God is good and loving, why is there evil and suffering in the world he created?

Maybe:

1. It's a mystery and paradox that we just have to accept by a leap of faith.

2. It's the result of the wrath of God.

3. It's because of Satan and his demons.

4. It's because God produces both good and evil.

Any or all of these might be true. But there are other options.

6.

Thriving

"The world needs a few rotten people
to make the sweetest mix."
- fictional character, Catherine [1]

"Without failure, no ethics."   - Simone de Beauvoir [2]

Option 5: Evil is Necessary for Good to Thrive

My husband, Ralph, and I have a favorite brand of coffee, which is roasted locally. We're so accustomed to drinking it that restaurant coffee is often disappointing. A few weeks ago, we had a fine, fancy restaurant meal and, again, a sadly lacking cup of coffee at the end. Trying to make the best of it, Ralph said, "Every once in awhile, you should drink a cup of bad restaurant coffee just to remind youself how good Portland Brew is."

It seems to be a principle of life that the bad makes us realize just how good the good is. Our world is full of contrasts. Some flavors we like, some we loathe. We want some fragrances to linger; we try to get rid of others. We stroke some textures, we recoil from others. It's the variety that makes life rich.

Besides, would we even recognize light without darkness? Would we know we're up if there were no down? Is it possible to experience the full delight of a glass of water unless we are thirsty? And – more to our point – can we perceive good without the knowledge of evil?

The knowledge of evil? Have we heard that somewhere before? Wasn't there once, long ago, a tree of the knowledge of good and . . . evil?

Think about it for a minute: The Bible never says Adam and Eve "fell." I'm not sure who first labeled it that way. But didn't God, being omniscient, know that Adam and Eve would eat from that tree? As I pointed out in another book, I know better than to leave candy in front of a two-year-old, tell him, "Don't eat that," and then leave the room. So maybe the tree was a set-up. Maybe Adam and Eve did exactly what God expected them to do. If so, what possible purpose could God have had in mind? Why would He want people to have the knowledge of both good and evil?

Could God have intended for Adam and Eve to know evil so they could see the extent of His goodness? Could He have wanted them to see how evil they could be, so they would know they were the creatures, not the Creator – so they would know they were not God? Maybe the only way humans can see the fullness of God's love is to see the evil at the other end of the spectrum. Maybe this was what the Tree of the Knowledge of Good and Evil was all about.

Ken Rideout, former missionary to Asia, puts it this way: "God, of course, does not sin. He is love, grace, mercy, and forgiveness. But these terms have meaning only when they are compared to sin, transgression, and dis-obedience. How do people come to know the gracious, merciful, forgiving heart of God? By going through a learning process to acquire a knowledge of good and evil. The tree . . . educated man so he could understand the goodness of God." [3]

In the book <u>Faust</u>, it's suggested "that knowledge and experience of evil are necessary for true virtue to flower."[4] In other words, if we can't choose evil, then can we truly say we've chosen good?

Maybe the world works on a principle that's like the dynamics of swimming. We can't move through water without exerting pressure on it and having it exert pressure back on us. Or think of cars. Our tires need to grab and push with the resistance of pavement under them. If our tires can't get traction, we simply spin our wheels. Or how about sand dunes? If you've ever tried to run up a sand dune, you know how it feels not to have resistance. Maybe evil is the resistance against which good operates in order to propel us down the road on the journey through life.

Speaking of journey, could God use evil to get us to look forward to our destination? In times of prosperity and peace, it's easy to center our lives around earning and spending and acquiring as if material possessions held the greatest value. Sometimes suffering is the icy blast that makes us long for God's hearth. Would we value the promise of the timeless dimension if we didn't know the heaviness of living in the time-bound world? Would we desire heaven if earth were perfect? Or maybe earth is perfect. Maybe perfection includes evil.

Another way of looking at this concept of "necessary evil" is expressed in the saying that we don't realize what we've got until it's gone. We don't appreciate what we have until we lose it. After a week of having a stopped-up nose, isn't the first clear breath marvelous? And when you finally recover from a knee injury, doesn't a healthy knee seem like one of the most amazing things? Our state has been suffering a drought, so every bit of water that comes from my faucet seems like a precious gift. The loss of a friend or family member can serve to give us a fresh appreciation for those we still have with us. An acquaintance of mine recently wrote a fictional book that deals with death. The main character remarked that if death hadn't been so close, she would not have treasured life as she did. [5]

Sometimes our values change because suffering or evil has put what's valuable in bold relief. Sometimes when we are confronted with evil, the gray areas recede, and right and wrong become obvious. In fact, some people believe that suffering serves to intimidate us into making the right choices and brings order to our lives. In other words, once we see the result of deceit and betrayal, or of rage and loss of self-control, we're motivated to "get our act together." One of the verses in Job shows Elihu counseling Job that way: ". . . it was to prevent you from getting into a life of evil that God sent this suffering" [6] Of course, as readers, we have the inside scoop on why Job was suffering, and Elihu's guess was not correct in Job's case. Still, it's an option to consider when looking at suffering as a whole.

Anyway, it makes sense to say that there's no way to become compassionate if there's no need for compassion. We can't be generous if no one needs anything. We can't show courage if there's no fear. And that brings us to our next option.

7.

Heroes

"And so from hour to hour, we ripe and ripe, and then, from hour to hour, we rot and rot, and thereby hangs a tale."
                                                        - Shakespeare[1]

Option 6: Suffering Can Turn Us Into Heroes

A train carrying toys and healthy food breaks down before it can take its cargo to the boys and girls on the other side of the mountain. Major catastrophe. No one will help. Until the little blue engine comes along. She's not very big. And she's never even been to the other side of the mountain. But she says, "I think I can. I think I can." And over the mountain she goes, to become the hero of the story.

I'm sure you recognized the childhood classic, <u>The Little Engine That Could</u>.[2] This same basic tale is retold in different guises all the time as writers show characters growing through painful circumstances. In fact, as I mentioned earlier, there is no story (at least none that anyone wants to read) if there's no conflict. If you're a novelist, you put a boulder in your protagonist's path. Then you grow the boulder into a hill. Then into a mountain. And as your protagonist climbs the mountain, you place a heavy pack on her back. Then she sprains her ankle. By the climax of the story, it looks as if there's no way she'll make it to the top of the mountain. But she does. What's more, she's changed by the journey, and we readers are deeply satisfied, perhaps even changed ourselves.

Conflict besets the hero's journey from begining to end. And thanks to evil and suffering, we all get to take the trip. We don't always call it a hero's journey. Sometimes we use other metaphors:

"Suffering is a crucible," some say. As metal is heated in a crucible to facilitate the removal of the dross in order to make the metal pure, so we are heated in the crucible of suffering, and we are purified as a result. "We know that suffering produces perseverance; perseverance, character, and character hope." [3]

Another metaphor is the diamond. As a diamond is cut into facets that perfectly reflect the light, so we are cut and shaped and formed by suffering so that we can perfectly reflect the Light.

A third metaphor has to do with gardening. As a gardener prunes a bush to make it grow fuller and stronger, so God prunes us through suffering so our lives will grow fuller and stronger. Actually, Jesus used this metaphor when He said, "I am the true vine, and my Father is the gardener. He cuts off every branch in me that bears no fruit, while every branch that does bear fruit he prunes so that it will be even more fruitful." [4]

One claim atheists make as proof that there's no God is that a perfect Creator would create perfection. If what He creates is imperfect, then the Creator is imperfect. Since suffering and evil are flaws, they say, there is no perfect God. But does the Perfect have to create perfection? What if God intentionally built imperfection into the world in order to perfect his creatures? Maybe life is that perfecting process.

There's a story in the Talmud in which Rabbi Akiva says, "Man was created imperfectly and it is he that is required to strive towards perfection." [5] We've already seen how pain gives us the chance to mature. C.S. Lewis quotes R. Havard, a doctor, who says, "Pain provides an opportunity for heroism; the opportunity is seized with surprising frequency." [6]

An example of this hero principle comes from another friend's recent novel. The main character is Jane, a teenager who has lost her arm in a shark attack. In the story, Andy, who has also lost the use of one arm, writes to Jane: "Life is funny, and sometimes it's easy to question why terrible things happen to good people, especially young folks like yourself. I believe there is a reason, though we may not see it for a long time. My hope for you is that someday, you feel that this accident has not ruined your life; only changed it from the original plan." [7] Andy is a hero. And by the end of the story, so is Jane, changed by suffering.

So are we God's story? The apostle Paul indicates that we are center-stage proof of God's wisdom. But proof to whom? It seems that we're proof to beings or quasi-beings in dimensions other than our own. "God's purpose was to show his wisdom in all its rich variety to all the rulers and authorities in the heavenly realms." This purpose, Paul says, is to bring all people of the world together.[8] Is it possible that the human family could find unity in working shoulder to shoulder to alleviate poverty and oppression and disease and injustice? Can we work through the friction, the challenges, the conflict, and the suffering inevitable in the human story and come out on the other side triumphant?

I know a missions pastor who has often traveled into the dangers of Afghanistan and Iraq. He has met people there who daily confront a type of suffering most of us see only on news programs. He says, "We become more beautiful by engaging the trouble, by confronting it." A woman who often visits persecuted Christians in China says, "The persecuted don't see themselves as victims. They're not bitter. Instead, they're loving and caring people." [9] For years, Elizabeth Kubler-Ross worked with dying people and their families. She commented, "People are like stained-glass windows. They sparkle and shine when the sun is out, but when the darkness sets in, their true beauty is revealed only if there is a light from within." [10]

We're not only given the opportunity to be heroes through our own suffering, but we're also given the opportunity to be heroes through our response to others who are suffering. Paul told the Corinthians that God comforts us in our troubles "so that we can comfort others." [11] Our own sufferings give us compassion for others, and the outworking of our compassion can make us heroic.

One woman told about caring for an aging grandfather, who had once been very alert and active. As she talked about the experience, she spoke as if caring for him was a gift to her. She was grateful. I've felt that myself. I once stayed a few hours with my husband's great-aunt, who had Alzheimer's disease. I had to help her go to the bathroom. She apologized for needing my help, but I told her it was my privilege to help her after she had spent her life helping others. And I meant it. As we dignify others in their suffering, we ourselves are given the gift of dignity. Is there any other way to get such a gift?

So perhaps the reason evil exists is to give us all the chance to become heroes. William Barclay wrote that Jesus "came not to make life easy but to make men great." [12] Maybe God tries to grow us up in wisdom and virtue and heroic integrity by challenging us to respond to the needs of the suffering world. That's one way to look at this good-God/suffering-world puzzle. But there's still another option.

8.

Dependence

"What have I done to you, O watcher of all humanity? Why have you made me your target?"

- Job [1]

Option 7: Evil Makes Us Depend on God

In the book of Job, suffering seems to be a kind of test and a proof to the accuser. Proof of what? That Job will not renounce God? That's obviously part of it. But perhaps it goes deeper – or higher as the case may be. I think it may have something to do with glory.

Glory is one of those words we toss around, usually in a religious context, without really thinking about what it means. Of course, sometimes we use it in a non-religious context like, "He had his moment of glory." Either way, glory is what happens when the spotlight shines on someone: an Olympic gold-medal winner, a movie star, a Pulitzer prize winner. Or God. What happens is, when the spotlight shines on them, they are revealed for who they are. In the case of the athlete or movie star or writer, the spotlight often shows the image their publicist has worked so hard (and at great expense) to perfect. In the case of God, when He has moments of glory, He reveals who He is. Or He allows us to reveal who He is. And since God is love [2], glory in the religious sense is the revealing of who God is in all His life-giving love.

Okay. I know you're asking what all this has to do with the suffering of the world. Maybe a lot. Trouble, challenges, pain, suffering, evil – all these press us to cope.

As we saw in the previous chapter, those who cope well are in many ways heroes. Sometimes they get the glory. Look at all the magazine articles and news programs that show how someone coped with a major life crisis. That person is in the spotlight. They are shown for who they are, at least in part. So they get the glory. Unless they say, "God got me through this." Then who gets the glory? God. God is revealed in all His life-giving love.

Now if there's anything God wants to communicate to people, it's His life-giving love. I think it's set up like this:

We have needs.
  God provides.
    We receive His provision gratefully.
      He is thus glorified (shown for who He is in all His life-giving love).
        People see God's life-giving love operating in our lives.
        They want it for their lives, too.

In this case, what is the function of suffering and evil? It causes us to feel our need for God and draws us to depend on Him. That way, when He works it out for good, He gets the glory. He is seen for who He truly is: Love in person.

Now to say evil and suffering make us depend on God is actually a strange way to put it. If there's a loving God, a caring Creator, then we are totally dependent on Him anyway, like it or not. Our very breath depends on His providing the air, not to mention our reliance on all the other life-sustaining and life-enriching elements God provides. So what this explanation of evil and suffering is really all about is us becoming aware of how finite, how fragile, how mortal we are. It's about us coming to terms with our complete inability to reverse some of life's dire situations. If the situation is going to change, it will change only with help from a much greater Source. And if the situation is not going to change, we will need Someone much stronger and wiser to see us through it.

For some people, the only time they pray is when situations get that grave. A friend says that only two things can crack open a hard heart: physical devastation, or intellectual, theological, and ethical devastation. Gerard Manley Hopkins, poet, priest, and writer, said, ". . . if we were not forced from time to time to feel our need of God and our dependence on him, we should most of us cease to pray to him and to thank him. If he did everything we should treat him as though he did nothing, . . . God desires nothing so much as that his creatures should have recourse to him." [3]

Now let me stir this concept around a bit. I realized this morning that I had been ungrateful in the midst of the drought we're going through in our state. I confessed my ingratitude in prayer and told God numerous things for which I'm grateful, including the water that still comes from my faucet. At the close of my prayer, I caught myself thinking, "Now that I've apologized, God will send rain." Really? Was this drought all my fault? And what if God doesn't send rain? What do I think then?

What happens when someone prays and prays but gets no answer? What if they depended on God and now feel He's let them down? Some people have become atheists because they felt that their prayers were all one-sided.

They could see no response from on high. And it's quite possible that someone told them they didn't pray hard enough, when in fact, they poured their heart out.

So, do our sufferings make us depend on God? Maybe. Maybe not. Depending on God may not make the evil and suffering go away. But the fact is, not depending on God doesn't make the evil and suffering go away either.

Maybe wrestling with the dark side is meant to show us that we're the creatures, not the Creator, that there are forces we don't understand, that we are not strong enough to win the struggle without God's life-giving love. C.S. Lewis put it this way: "The creature's illusion of self-sufficiency must, for the creature's sake, be shattered. . ." [4] Julian of Norwich expressed the same thought quite pointedly. To her, suffering was intended "to prevent the damage that would be done to us by pomp and vainglory." [5]

But there are questions that go along with this option. One questions deals with degrees of suffering. I've seen godly people who already depend on the Lord go through unrelieved physical suffering, and I've seen many unbelievers live relatively suffering-free lives. You would think it would be just the opposite. Unbelievers would need to learn to rely on God through suffering.

A second question is: If the purpose of suffering is to make us turn to God, then what is our role in alleviating suffering? If we try to diminish someone's pain, are we taking away their God-given opportunity to depend on Him? When chloroform was first used as an anesthetic to help women through the pain of childbirth, some people were incensed. They called chloroform "a decoy of Satan, apparently opening itself to bless women, but in the end hardening them, and robbing God of the deep, earnest cries, that should arise to him in time of trouble." [6]

A third question concerns the suffering of innocent children. Certainly I would suffer emotionally if my baby were suffering physically. I might be strengthened in my resolve to depend on God. But would God make my child suffer so that I might learn to rely on Him? That doesn't seem fair or right or loving. So, while this option is viable, it leaves us with more questions.

9.

Free Will

"Liberty is so holy a thing that God was forced to permit Evil, that it might exist."

- Acton [1]

An old Cherokee tale relates a discussion between a chief and his grandson:

"The battle is between two wolves," said Grandfather. "One is evil. It is anger, envy, sorrow, regret, greed, arrogance, self-pity, guilt, resentment, inferiority, lies, false pride, superiority and ego. The other is Good. It is peace, love, hope, serenity, humility, kindness, joy, benevolence, empathy, generosity, truth, compassion and faith."

"Which wolf wins?" asked the grandson.

"The one you feed," Grandfather replied. [2]

Option 8: We Suffer Because of Free Will

Personal responsibility. Choice. Free will. This is perhaps the most commonly held and widely-known answer to the good-God/suffering-world dilemma. "We believe," writes Lesslie Newbigin, "that in his creation of the world God gave it a measure of independence and to that extent limited his own freedom." [3] Could evil be the price God paid for our free will?

One explanation for free will goes like this: If God, being love, wanted to create beings who could love (each other as well as Him), He had to give them free will and take the risk that they might choose not to love. I find that explanation believable because, from a human standpoint, we want someone to love us by choice, not because they have no choice. A forced "love" doesn't seem like love at all. So if this same desire was in God's mind, He obviously decided that creating us with free will was worth the risk.

C.S. Lewis points out that if we try to eliminate the suffering that free will necessarily entails, we eliminate life. [5] So if free will is a good that God made, and if suffering is a side-effect of free will, does that mean that suffering is good too? How does that support the claim that God is love? Maybe philosopher Alvin Plantinga has the answer. He said, "An all-loving, all powerful, all knowing Being could permit as much evil as He pleased without forfeiting His claim to being all loving, so long as for every evil state of affairs He permits there is an accompanying greater good." [5] And if we look around, we find abundant good in the world. In fact, as heroes, we have a chance to add more good.

But there may be more to free will than what's attributed to humans. Let's revisit the idea of the Dark Side for a minute. If free will allows us to choose evil, perhaps free will allowed spirits to choose evil as well. That was one of our theories about the accuser. Sylvia Browne has an interesting perspective on this. While I don't totally buy into her beliefs, I do think she has a valid point about free will as it relates to the good-God/evil-world question. She believes that God did not create evil. Otherwise, part of Him would have to be evil, which she does not believe. So she says some spirits used their free will to reject God. She writes, "God never turns away from anyone, but He won't stop anyone from turning away from Him. . . . Yes, there are consequences for rejecting Him and His love. But He doesn't doom those who refuse to reciprocate that love and would rather live in darkness. They doom themselves." [6]

This, in fact, is what author Jaroslav Pelikan points out when he writes, "Augustine says God does not rape; God woos, and therefore God will take his chances on winning or losing and will finally prefer to let someone be lost rather than to interfere with the sacredness of the human person." [7]

Our freedom to choose seems to be a sign of just how highly God values humans. It's God's loving generosity at work. Professor Hillel Levine puts it this way:

"God, as a very precious gift, gives people freedom . . . People are free to create the Auschwitzes. People are free to create the Beethoven symphonies." [8]

But how about cancer, back problems, crippling disease? Is that kind of suffering due to free will? Some people would say yes. Carlos Annacondia, an evangelist from Argentina says he estimates that 70% of all sickness and other troubles plague us because we don't forgive. We live in complaint and rancor, resentment and bitterness. "God forbids nothing," says Annacondia. "You can do anything you want. But if you move out of His love, you will suffer. God doesn't want you to suffer." So God tells us how to live a life of health. He tells us to forgive. Annacondia says that all over the world, cripples walk again and cancers disappear when people choose to forgive. [9]

Now I have to admit that, while I have no reason to doubt the evangelist, I have not seen this type of healing. But Rabbi Edwin H. Friedman has a similar observation. He attributes many of our health problems to our choice to see ourselves as victims. He tells the story of a pastor who had relationship problems with his wife, with his father (who was already dead), and with his mother. Then the pastor got cancer. After counseling, the pastor decided to let go of his past. And his cancer went into remission. [10] A victim sees him or herself as being wronged. Guess what that usually includes? Unforgiveness. So maybe a great deal of our suffering, as far as sickness goes, is truly our fault, brought about by our free will choice to hang onto bitterness and resentment.

What about children who suffer? This is one of the most disturbing questions of theodicy. In the ninth and last circle of "Inferno," Dante indicates that he believes that the suffering of children is a by-product of the radical evil of adults.[11] Which, of course, brings us back to the free will of those adults.

And what about natural disasters? Believe it or not, there's a link to free will here as well. One possibility is that the spirit powers that chose the Dark Side disrupted and twisted God's original creation. But C.S. Lewis gives us another possibility: "I am going to submit that not even Omnipotence could create a society of free souls without at the same time creating a relatively independent and 'inexorable' Nature." [12] Nature is what it is and does what it does. Gravity is good, but if you defy gravity and step off a cliff, the result is not good. Fire is good. But the same qualities that make it good and useful are also dangerous.

From another perspective, not all of us are happy with the same state of nature. I may pray for rain to water my newly planted Japanese maple, when at the same time, my neighbor is praying for a sunny day for the school picnic. One of us is going to be disappointed.

Of course, that problem pales to insignificance when it comes to tsunamis and hurricanes and volcanoes. Maybe the seismologist is delighted to study the effects of tectonic shifts, or a storm-tracker gets a high out of chasing a tornado or flying into the eye of a hurricane, but most people focus only on the devastation these events leave in their wake. Still, we could attribute at least the weather catastrophes to past and present free-will choices that may cause major climate change.

So . . . is the answer free will? Maybe. Are there any other options left?

10.

Pain and Love

"The web of our life is of a mingled yarn,
good and ill together."

- Shakespeare [1]

Option 9: Pain Lets God Show How Much He Loves Us

Let's go back to the idea of "story" that we looked at earlier. Like me, you may have read and/or heard many of the sacred stories and writings of other religions. If so, you know that the Bhagadvad Gita contains many beautiful, uplifting praise passages. The Tao and Qur'an can be inspiring. Zen writings have a deep, spiritual quality. But as a writer, I must say that among all these writings, the Bible is unique. It contains, truly, the most cohesive and beautiful story I've ever read.

Lesslie Newbigin says that the Bible story invites us to "indwell" it. ". . . we live IN the biblical story as part of the community whose story it is . . . and from within that indwelling try to understand and cope with the events of our time and the world about us and so carry the story forward." [2]

I love the simplicity of that perspective: carry the story forward. And yet, we've let our opinions grow up around Christianity until our belief system is like an onion. We've taken the core of the story and added layer upon layer upon layer until the world sees only the outside layers of peripheral issues that divide Christians from one another. But if we peel the layers off, we find the core is still there. (Warning: Peeling an onion may cause you to cry. I trust that you get the analogy.)

What's at the core? Jesus.

You knew that was coming, didn't you? It sounds so cliche, it rolls right off our minds. So let's challenge our minds for a minute and try to gain a different perspective, maybe find a more meaningful way to see the core. Let's start with some questions.

Is it right for me to steal from you?

Is it right for me to abuse you?

Is it right for me to murder you?

All people, even non-Christians, will answer "no" to each of those questions. Why? Because all people know what perfect, unconditional love is. Not that all people have experienced it. But all people know how they should be treated. And all people know when they're not being treated that way.

Do you love perfectly?

Does anyone love perfectly?

All people, even non-Christians, will answer "no" to those questions. There's an inner standard by which we measure our fellow-humans. (If we don't have a double-standard, we measure ourselves by it too.) What is the standard? Perfect, unconditional love. If we're honest with ourselves, each of us knows we don't measure up. None of us loves perfectly.

But then, we're the creation, not the Creator. By definition, the Creator is greater than what He created. So He would have to be greater than the most respected, most honorable, noblest attitude a human can conceive of. What is the greatest, noblest attitude of one human toward another? Unconditional love.

What's the greatest act of love one human can show another? Researchers who study moral development say the highest stage of morality is self-sacrificial love.

Novelists and screenwriters know that the way to impact the hearts of their readers or their audience is to show a character sacrificing himself or herself for the good of others.

So if the Most High God wants to communicate the depths of His love clearly to His creation, how will He do it? He'll have to do it in a way that we humans will understand. He'll have to use our language. Our body language. He'll have to do what we know the noblest human would do: give up his or her own life for someone else. Usually if a human goes that far, it will be for the benefit of friends or family. In God's case, He gave His life for His enemies as well.

How does this apply to evil in the world? "The world is a dance," wrote C.S. Lewis, "in which good, descending from God, is disturbed by evil arising from the creatures, and the resulting conflict is resolved by God's own assumption of the suffering nature which evil produces." [3]

Let's turn this concept slightly and view it from another angle. Think back to the standard of perfect, unconditional love that all humanity senses. We all know we can't live up to it. But God is Perfect Love. He can live up to it; He IS the standard. Perfect, Unconditional Love does not sit comfortably in His dimension, watching us try and try again and ultimately fail. No, if Perfect Love wants us to measure up, He becomes human. He measures up for us. He LIVES for us. Perfectly. Only then does He die for us. He bequeaths His Perfect Love to us, so that we might, in Him, indwell Perfect Love and that Perfect Love might indwell us. [4]

God became human to do for us what we can't do for ourselves, so that we who condemn ourselves for consistently failing to live up to the standard, can rise from our failures, move forward, and truly LIVE. Uncondemned.

So what's at the core? God's Perfect Love incarnate. Jesus.

Now, I believe all that with my whole heart. But do I believe evil and suffering exist just so God can show us how much He loves us by suffering and dying as a human? Is that the whole picture? Possibly. If God intended for us to have the knowledge of good and evil, then it seems an appropriate climax: First God lets us see and experience the horror of evil and shows us that not only are we inadequate to deal with it, but what's worse, we're the perpetrators of it. Then He absorbs that evil into Himself, nullifies it, and erases its control over us.

But we still have daily pains, even those of us who believe in Jesus. All humans still suffer. Evil is still around. "What is clear . . ." writes Lesslie Newbigin, "is that the powers (of evil) have been disarmed but not destroyed. They are put under the supreme dominion of Christ by what he has done on the cross, but they still exist. We have to wrestle with them." [5]

I don't know about you, but I'm still left with Why?

11.

Turning Evil Into Good

"All the death that ever was, set next to life,
would scarcely fill a cup."
- Frederick Buechner [1]

Option 10: Suffering Shows How God Can Turn Evil Into Good

Novelist Hugh Nissenson says that for years he quarreled with God about death. "God said, 'Do justice,' and I believed it. But cancer and Auschwitz made me pray, 'Practice what you preach, Oh Lord.' My love for Him, which was mixed with fear, became hate. I gave up my faith. I hate the idea that a just and loving God allows cells to metastasize and men to make gas chambers." [2] Nissenson couldn't reconcile a good God with an evil world, so he became an atheist.

My friend Ken Rideout tells about a lunch meeting he had with an atheist some years ago in Jakarta, Indonesia. In the course of their conversation, the atheist said, "I have lived a long time and have seen a lot in this world. I have seen killings, wars, endless injustices, and cruelty. Right outside the door of this restaurant, people do not have enough to eat, and here we sit in luxury, enjoying ourselves. If there were a God, he would not create or tolerate a world like this. Therefore, there is not a God. If there were a God, he would not be worthy of my respect."

Ken took a piece of paper and drew a line down the middle to make two columns. At the top of the first column, he wrote, "The World." Under that, he listed evils in the world:

<u>The World</u>
War
Cruelty
Adultery
Lying
Cheating
Rape
Murder

At the top of the second column, Ken wrote, "God." He said, "Let's say that there is no God." He drew an X through God's name in the second column. "Has anything changed now that we have taken God out of the picture?"

"No," said the man.

"Without God in the picture, who is to blame for the evil that is in the world: the lying, murder, adultery, rape, war, and so forth?" asked Ken.

"People," said the man.

So Ken wrote "People" in the column under the crossed-out "God."

<u>The World</u>	~~God~~
War	People
Cruelty	
Adultery	
Lying	
Cheating	
Rape	
Murder	

"Why blame people for all these evils?" asked Ken. "Why hold people responsible? The tiger eats the deer. The cat eats the mouse. The landslide wipes out an entire village. Why don't we blame the tiger, the cat, and the landslide in the same way we blame people?"

"Because people are responsible beings with wills," said the atheist. "People choose their actions."

"Are you sure people are responsible?" Ken asked.

"Yes," said the man.

"So let's put God back in the picture," said Ken. "Why blame God for what you say people have freely chosen to do?" [3]

In the bleak picture atheists paint, it looks like there's no hope. Unless they're willing to put God back into the picture. That brings up the tenth option for explaining the presence of evil: to provide an environment in which God can show how He turns evil into good.

How can God turn evil into good?

Here's a historical example. By the late fourth century, Christianity had been accepted and legalized in Rome. But gladiators still fought in the arena, and crowds still gathered to cheer their bloody deaths. These were not Christians fighting beasts anymore; instead, they were men Rome had conquered in battle, now forced to fight each other. One day, a Christian monk named Telemachus, a newcomer to Rome, followed the crowd into the stadium. When he saw what was about to happen, he was appalled. He rushed into the ring and stood between the two gladiators to stop the fight. The gladiators shoved the monk out of the way, and the crowd shouted at him to let the men fight. But Telemachus pushed himself back between the two gladiators. The commander of the games yelled his order, and one of the gladiators struck the monk dead. A hush came over the crowd. That day, the gladiatorial games ended. [4] A hideous death. A great good.

But that's ancient history, you say. Then look at Beethoven's life. Researchers recently discovered evidence that the great composer lived with lead poisoning in his system, which means he was probably in terrible pain. Every day. But the music he produced out of that pain ranks among the most inspiring and uplifting in the world.

Still too distant in the past? Think back to a more recent event, the martyrdom of Jim Elliot in Ecuador. Consider the impact for good that his wife, Elizabeth, has since made in that nation and around the world.

Let's go with a very recent, unpublished, unsung event. Not long ago, a friend's daughter-in-law died suddenly. My friend spent a week with her grieving son and his four children. In an e-mail to me, she wrote, "It's a paradoxically tough and beautiful time. Lots of pain and lots of love."

Remember the twenty-third psalm, written by the shepherd David? He had fought off lions and bears and who knows what other dangers. He wrote:

"The Lord is my shepherd;
    I have everything I need.
He lets me rest in green meadows;
    he leads me beside peaceful streams.
    He renews my strength.
He guides me along right paths,
    bringing honor to his name.
Even when I walk
    through the dark valley of death,
I will not be afraid,
    for you are close beside me.
Your rod and your staff
    protect and comfort me.
You prepare a feast for me
    in the presence of my enemies." [5]

A feast. In the presence of enemies. In the presence of sickness? In the presence of natural disaster? In the presence of terrorism? Nissenson hasn't found the feast. He says, "What I now realize, of course, is that I make a religion of my atheism. And also of my art. All my work expresses my insatiable adolescent longing to believe in something enduring." [6] Does he call it an "adolescent" longing because he has crossed out GOD? Is that why he can't validate that longing? Is that why he thinks his longing will never be fulfilled?

But notice: He still longs, like all human beings. Why? Maybe deep down, we know that cancers and gas chambers are perversions. They're at the deep end of all that's wrong. But we'd have no basis to even think such a thing if we didn't also know that there is another end of the spectrum. There is right. And there is good. Great good. Lasting good. And, no, that's not called adolescence. That's called hope. Hope in a Good Shepherd who serves a feast in the presence of our enemies. Can that feast ever be found without Him?

So do evil and suffering exist so that God can show us how He can change bad into good? Maybe.

12.

Intention

"God does not play dice with the world. . . .
God is subtle, but he is not malicious."
- Albert Einstein [1]

Option 11: Intention

One of Tolkien's points in <u>The Lord of the Rings</u> is that "evil's triumph is not final," and what's more, it tends to destroy itself. [2] That's a hopeful way to look at it, and one that we might keep in mind as we review our options for explaining the good-God/suffering-world conundrum. If you didn't have an affinity for one of these options before you began this book, perhaps you were drawn to one or more as you read.

1. It's a mystery, a paradox.
2. It's the wrath of God.
3. It's caused by Satan and demons.
4. God produces both good and evil.
5. Evil is necessary for good to thrive.
6. It's meant to bring us to depend on God.
7. It's meant to turn us all into heroes.
8. It's the result of free will.
9. It's so God can show his full love.
10. It's to show how God can turn evil into good.

I have one more thought on the subject. It all seems to me to have a great deal to do with intention. What does God intend? What is His purpose for the world in the first place? What is His purpose for putting us here? What is God's purpose in the grand, cosmic scheme of things?

While we have clues to the answers to these questions, much of what we know is clouded in mystery. We're like children trying to conceive of what it's like to be a grown-up. It's all there, acted out in front of us, but we have no real idea what it's like.

One Christian creed ventures to tell us what our purpose is:

> The chief end of man is to glorify God
> and enjoy him forever.

John Piper suggests changing that creed by substituting one word:

> The chief end of man is to glorify God
> *by* enjoying him forever. [3]

I like that. These two versions of the creed might point to some of our options. But I want to explore further. Let's take a speed-run through the Bible and see what we come up with regarding God's intention, His purpose.

"Let us make people in our image, to be like ourselves. They will be masters over all life – the fish in the sea, the birds in the sky, and all the livestock, wild animals, and small animals." Genesis 1:26

Purpose? Guardianship of creation (This is thematically restated two verses later and again to Noah after the flood, Genesis 9:1)

"All the families of the earth will be blessed through you."
Genesis 12:3
>   **Purpose?** Ferry God's blessings to everyone (This was
>   said to Abraham, but inherited by us,
>   Galatians 3:29)

"God's purpose . . . is that people should fear him."
Ecclesiastes 3:14
>   **Purpose?** Respect for God ("Fear" here means deep
>   reverence and respect. It has to do with
>   God's glory.)

"All who claim me as their God will come, for I have made
them for my glory. It was I who created them." Isaiah 43:7
>   **Purpose?** God's glory

"You have been chosen to know me, believe in me, and
understand that I alone am God." Isaiah 43:10
>   **Purpose?** Know, believe in, understand who God is.
>   (That's glory.)

"He made the world to be lived in, not to be a place of
empty chaos." Isaiah 45:18
>   **Purpose?** Life, fullness

"For the Lord has planted them like strong and graceful
oaks for his own glory." Isaiah 61:3
>   **Purpose?** For His glory

Jesus prayed, "Father, I want these whom you've given me
to be with me, so they can see my glory." John 17:24
>   **Purpose?** For His glory

"There is only one God, the Father, who created everything, and we exist for him." 1 Corinthians 8:6
Purpose? For God

"His unchanging plan has always been to adopt us into his own family by bringing us to himself through Jesus Christ. And this gave him great pleasure." Ephesians 1:5
Purpose? Be God's family

"And this is his (God's) plan: At the right time he will bring everything together under the authority of Christ – everything in heaven and on earth." Ephesians 1:10
Purpose? Unity of heaven and earth

"God's purpose was that we . . . should praise our glorious God." Ephesians 1:12
Purpose? God's glory

". . . so God can always point to us as examples of the incredible wealth of his favor and kindness . . ." Ephesians 2:7
Purpose? To show God's favor and kindness (That's glory.)

"For we are God's masterpiece. He has created us anew in Christ Jesus, so that we can do the good things he planned for us long ago." Ephesians 2:10
Purpose? Perpetuate good

"His purpose was to make peace between Jews and [non-Jews] . . . And this is the secret plan: The [non-Jews] have an equal share with the Jews in all the riches inherited by God's children." Ephesians 3:6
Purpose? Unity

"He called you into his Kingdom to share his glory." 1 Thessalonians 2:12
   Purpose? To share God's glory

"He died for us so that we can live with him forever." 1 Thessalonians 5:10
   Purpose? To live with God

". . . that was [God's] plan long before the world began – to show his love and kindness to us through Christ Jesus." 2 Timothy 1:9
   Purpose? For God to show his love (That's glory.)

"You are . . . [God's] very own possession. This is so you can show others the goodness of God, for he called you out of the darkness into his wonderful light." 1 Peter 2:9
   Purpose? To show God's goodness (That's glory.)

"You (God) created everything,
       and it is for your pleasure that
       they exist and were created." Revelation 4:11
   Purpose? For God's pleasure

Okay, this is not an exhaustive study, (aren't you glad!) but it gives us a good idea of God's purpose and our purpose, and it seems to point to God's glory, revealing God for who He is in all His life-giving love. And I've merely scratched the surface of what's said about glorifying God. So it seems that as we consider our explanations for evil, we'd be wise to make sure the option(s) we choose shows God in all His life-giving love.

Whatever we may say about the Why of evil, the simple fact is that evil exists and we must grapple with it. How? If God is greater than evil, and if He keeps emphasizing that He wants all people to know Him for His life-giving love, then maybe we should deal with evil by showing God's life-giving love. Jesus said the most important thing is to "'Love the Lord your God with all your heart, all your soul, all your mind, and all your strength.' The second is equally important: 'Love your neighbor as yourself.'" [4]

So I say, suffering or no suffering, our purpose is to learn and practice love. Are you sick? Learn and practice love. Are you healthy? Learn and practice love. Are you rich? Learn and practice love. Are you poor? Learn and practice love. Don't know what to do? Go for what brings life. Go for what spreads unconditional, other-centered love. If we all spent our lives learning and practicing love, can you imagine how far that would go toward eradicating evil?

Each of us is a living, breathing embassy of God's love here in our time-bound world. We are conduits of Christ's presence. And "when Christ is there the storm becomes a calm, the tumult becomes a peace, what cannot be done is done, the unbearable becomes bearable, and men pass the breaking point and do not break." [5] Why? Because in the presence of evil, God, in His life-giving love, provides a feast – exactly what we need when we need it. So "in the valley of the shadow of death, I will fear no evil." [6]

Which of the options we've explored is correct? Maybe all of them. Any one of our options gets God off the hook. Not that He needs our help in that department. God being God, I expect there will be plenty of surprises when we cross into His dimension. The point is, there are reasons – plausible reasons – for why a good, loving God might allow evil in this world. I don't plan to throw away my belief in God simply because I can't explain evil. N.T. Wright says, "turning away from the living God . . . is the spiritual equivalent of a diver cutting off his own breathing tube." [7] And I want to breathe.

A young girl once asked me why God is invisible. I answered, "He's not. It's just that our eyes are not sharp enough to see him." I figure that if humans can't hear some of the frequencies dogs can hear, humans probably can't see some of the sights there are to see. Like the spiritual realm. So why doesn't God let us see Him? Why doesn't He explain Himself more to our liking? Maybe it's because He knows how a search and a mystery intrigue us. It certainly keeps us thinking about Him. Or maybe it's because He knows our human bodies and psyches can't handle the dynamics of the spiritual world. Or maybe it's because when we humans come to understand a thing, we immediately set about trying to control it.

That brings us full circle. God is God, and even with all our possible options listed, questions remain. There will always be some mystery. When my sons were young, they'd often get into deep theological Why's right at bedtime. I remember my husband explaining as much as he knew how to explain, then he would say, "I think we've hit the wall." But the search is worth the time. Maybe it allows us to stay up a little bit later.

I trust that you've argued with some of my points. You've probably offered some "yeah, but's." That's good. You're still climbing the mountain, just as I am. But I must confess that in the end, I don't put my trust in a definitive

Why anyway. I put my trust in a Person called Love. A Person who has earned my trust. A Person who has always brought me through every rockslide, every fog bank, every moonless night I've encountered so far in my journey up the mountain. Without hesitation, I can recommend Him as a true and competent guide.

> "There are three things that will endure –
> faith, hope, and love –
> and the greatest of these is
> love." [8]

Footnotes and Works Cited

<u>Chapter One</u>
    1. Quoted in Billy Graham, <u>Death and the Life After</u>. (Dallas: Word, 1987, rev. 2001) 3.
    2. N.T. Wright, <u>Evil and the Justice of God</u>. (Downer's Grove, IL: InterVarsity, 2006) 24.
    3. James W. Fowler. <u>Stages of Faith: The Psychology of Human Development and the Quest for Meaning</u>. (San Francisco: Harper, 1981).

<u>Chapter Two</u>
    1. A.L. Kennedy, "Genesis." <u>Killing the Buddha</u>. Comp. Peter Manseau and Jeff Sharlet. (New York: Simon and Schuster, 2004) 20.
    2. Susan Beth Pfeffer, <u>Life As We Knew It</u>. (San Diego: Harcourt, 2006) 114.
    3. Luke Timothy Johnson, <u>The Story of the Bible</u> tape set. (Chantilly, Virginia: Teaching Company, 2006) lecture 22.
    4. Daniel J. Boorstin, <u>The Seekers</u>. (New York: Random House, 1998) 85.
    5. Mary Oliver, <u>Why I Wake Early</u>. (Boston: Beacon Press, 2004) 65.
    6. Randall Niles, <u>What Happened to Me?</u>: Reflections of a Journey. (New York: iUniverse, 2004) 99.
    7. Bruse Willems, producer, <u>This Is Who I Am</u>. (Elgin, IL: Harbinger, nd).
    8. Daniel J. Boorstin, <u>The Seekers</u>. (New York: Random House, 1998) 14.

9. Malcolm David Eckel, <u>Great World Religions: Buddhism</u> tape set. (Chantilly, Virginia: Teaching Company, 2003) lecture five.

10. John 11:50, NIV

11. Ralph C. Wood, <u>The Gospel According to Tolkein</u>. (Louisville: Westminster, 2003) 61.

<u>Chapter Three</u>

1. As quoted by Lee Strobel. <u>The Case for Faith: A Journalist Investigates the Toughest Objections to Christianity</u>. (Grand Rapids, MI: Zondervan, 2000) 15.

2. Mark W. Muiesse, <u>Great World Religions: Hinduism</u> tape set. (Chantilly, Virginia, 2003).lecture eleven.

3. Don Belt, "Struggle for the Soul of Pakistan," <u>National Geographic</u>, Sept. 2007: 32-59.

4. For a review that includes this fact plus a review of the new book <u>God's Judgments</u>,   see Stephen H. Webb, "The CT Review," <u>Christianity Today</u>, August 2007: 55-56.

5. Robert C. Solomon. <u>The Passions: Philosophy and the Intelligence of Emotions</u> tape set. (Chantilly, Virginia, 2006) lecture eight.

6. Romans 12:19, NRSV, quoting Deuteronomy 32:35

7. Proverbs 25:21

8. Hebrews 12:7, NIV

9. C.S. Lewis. <u>The Problem of Pain</u>. (San Francisco: HarperCollins, 1940, 1996) 93.

<u>Chapter Four</u>

 1. Ken Rideout, <u>The Truth You Know You Know</u>. (Nashville: NDX, 2005) 183.

 2. N.T. Wright refers to Satan as quasi-personal in <u>Evil and the Justice of God</u>. (Downer's Grove, IL: InterVarsity, 2006) 81.

 3. R.H. Charles, trans., <u>The Book of Enoch</u>. (Mineola, NY: Dover, 1893, 2007 ed.) 89.

 4. Acts 10:38

 5. Luke 13:15, 16

 6. Matthew 4, Mark 1
   Matthew 16:23
   Mark 4:15
   Luke 22:3, Mark 1:23-26
   Matthew 8:16
   Matthew 25:41
   Luke 22:31
   Matthew 13:39
   Luke 10:18
   John 8:44
   Acts 13:10

 7. John 12:32
   1 John 3:8

 8. Habakkuk 1:2 ff

 9. John 3:17

<u>Chapter Five</u>

 1. Julian of Norwich (c. 1342-1416), <u>Revelations of Divine Love</u>. Trans. Elizabeth Spearing. (New York: Penguin, 1998) 69.

2. C.S. Lewis. <u>The Problem of Pain</u>. (San Francisco: HarperCollins, 1940, 1996) 63.

3. Mark Muesse, <u>Religions of the Axial Age</u> tape set. (Chantilly, Virginia, 2007) lecture eighteen.

4. For a fuller and wiser discussion of this, see <u>Evil and the Justice of God</u>. (Downer's Grove, IL: InterVarsity, 2006) 21.

5. Daniel J. Boorstin, <u>The Seekers</u>. (New York: Random House, 1998) 216.

6. 1 Corinthians 15:26, NIV

7. Ralph C. Wood, <u>The Gospel According to Tolkein</u>. (Louisville: Westminster, 2003) 67.

8. Wood, 20

<u>Chapter Six</u>

1. Karen Cushman, <u>Catherine, Called Birdy</u>. (New York: HarperCollins, 1994) 39.

2. Quoted by Zadie Smith. "Fail Better." <u>The Guardian</u>, 20 January 2007.<http://www. books.guardian. co.uk/review/story/0..1988887,00.html>.

3. Ken Rideout, <u>The Truth You Know You Know</u>. (Nashville: NDX, 2005) 61.

4. Mentioned by Wood in <u>The Gospel According to Tolkein</u>, 53. Wood points out that Tolkein rejects this Faustian idea.

5. Martine Leavitt. <u>Keturah and Lord Death.</u> (Asheville: Front Street, 2006).

6. Job 36:21

Chapter Seven

    1. Shakespeare, <u>As You Like It</u>, Act II, sc 7.

    2. Watty Piper, <u>The Little Engine That Could</u>. (New York: Platt and Munk, 1954).

    3. Romans 5:3, 4, NIV

    4. John 15:1, 2

    5. Isaiah M. Gafni, <u>Great World Religions: Judaism</u> tape set. (Chantilly, Virginia, 2003) lecture seven.

    6. C.S. Lewis. <u>The Problem of Pain</u>. (San Francisco: HarperCollins, 1940, 1996) 162.

    7. Kelly Bingham, <u>Shark Girl</u>. (Cambridge: Candlewick, 2007) 220.

    8. Ephesians 3:1-13, NLT

    9. Keeping secret the names of those quoted may be important, so I'll not reveal their identity.

    10. Quote found in Isabella catalog, summer 2007.

    11. 2 Corinthians 1:4, NLT

    12. William Barclay, <u>The Gospel of Mark</u>. (Philadelphia: Westmister, 1975 ed.) 202.

Chapter Eight

    1. Job 7:2

    2. 1 John 4:8

    3. Gerard Manley Hopkins. <u>Mortal Beauty, God's Grace</u>. Ed. John F. Thornton and Susan B. Varenne. (New York: Random House, 2003) 160.

    4. C.S. Lewis. <u>The Problem of Pain</u>. (San Francisco: HarperCollins, 1940, 1996) 96.

5. Julian of Norwich (c. 1342-1416), <u>Revelations of Divine Love</u>. Trans. Elizabeth Spearing. (New York: Penguin, 1998) 79.

6. William Barclay, <u>The Gospel of Mark</u>. (Philadelphia: Westmister, 1975 ed.) 127.

Chapter Nine

1. Quoted in Boorstin, <u>The Seekers</u>. (New York: Random House, 1998) 239.

2. Told in <u>Isabella</u> catalog, Summer 2007, unattributed.

3. Lesslie Newbigin, <u>The Gospel in a Pluralist Society</u>. (Grand Rapids: Eerdmas, 1989) 71.

4. C.S. Lewis. <u>The Problem of Pain</u>. (San Francisco: HarperCollins, 1940, 1996) 25.

5. Quoted by Randall Niles. "The Problem of Evil." 3 September 2007. <www.allaboutgod.com/problem-of-evil.htm>

6. Sylvia Browne, <u>The Other Side and Back</u>. (New York: Penguin, 1999) 180, 181.

7. Jaroslav Pelikan, "Writing as a Means of Grace." <u>Going on Faith</u>. Ed. William Zinsser (New York: Marlowe, 1999) 127.

8. Hillel Levine, "In Search of Sugihara." <u>Going on Faith</u>, 71

9. Carlos Annacondia. Sermon. Belmont Church, Nashville, TN. 26 Aug. 2007.

10. Edwin H. Friedman, <u>Generation to Generation</u>. (New York: Guildford, 1985) 304.

11. William R. Cook and Ronald B. Herzman, <u>Dante's Divine Comedy</u> tape set. (Chantilly, Virginia, 2003) lecture eleven.

12. C.S. Lewis. <u>The Problem of Pain</u>. (San Francisco: HarperCollins, 1940, 1996) 19.

13. Lewis, 23.

<u>Chapter Ten</u>

1. Shakespeare, <u>All's Well that Ends Well</u>, Act IV, sc 3.

2. Lesslie Newbigin, <u>The Gospel in a Pluralist Society</u>. (Grand Rapids: Eerdmas, 1989) 99.

3. C.S. Lewis. <u>The Problem of Pain</u>. (San Francisco: HarperCollins, 1940, 1996) 80.

4. John 15:4

5. Newbigin, 204.

<u>Chapter Eleven</u>

1. Frederick Buechner, "Faith and Fiction." <u>Going on Faith</u>. Ed. William Zinsser (New York: Marlowe, 1999) 63.

2. Hugh Nissenson, "A Sense of the Holy." <u>Going on Faith</u>. Ed. William Zinsser (New York: Marlowe, 1999) 160, 161.

3. N. Kenneth Rideout, <u>The Truth You Know You Know</u>. (Nashville: NDX, 2005) 22-24.

4. This story can be found in William Barclay, <u>The Gospel of Mark</u>. (Philadelphia: Westmister, 1975 ed.) 203-205.

5. Psalm 23:1-5, NLT

6. Nissenson, 160, 161.

Chapter Twelve

1. Quoted in Boorstin, <u>The Seekers</u>. (New York: Random House, 1998) 258.

2. Ralph C. Wood, <u>The Gospel According to Tolkein</u>. (Louisville: Westminster, 2003) 75, 58.

3. John Piper, <u>Desiring God</u>. (Sisters, OR: Multnomah, 1996) 15.

4. Mark 12:30, 31

5. William Barclay, <u>The Gospel of Mark</u>. (Philadelphia: Westmister, 1975 ed.) 161.

6. Psalm 23:4

7. N.T. Wright, <u>Evil and the Justice of God</u>. (Downer's Grove, IL: InterVarsity, 2006) 109.

8. 1 Corinthians 13:13, NLT

www.ingramcontent.com/pod-product-compliance
Lightning Source LLC
Chambersburg PA
CBHW061745050726
47598CB00002B/593